Animal Alphabet

A

Baboon

Buffalo

Bee

C

Bear

B

My First ABC Book.

My Name Is _______________

Note to Parents

This is a wonderful ABC animal and insect alphabet book for toddlers from age 1 through pre-school toddlers and kindergarten kids to first-grade students. Your toddler and kids will have fun and learn a lot about the alphabet and the nicely illustrated animals.

This book contains the alphabet, the corresponding animal illustration to each letter, and a letter-shaped animal. In addition, there is a short narration about each letter and the related animals that begin with the alphabet.

You will have to start by reading the book to your toddler initially. This way, they will learn something interesting and be able to match the animals to the letters playfully and later be able to read the book on their own after hearing the narrations several times. Especially when they like this book, pictures, and stories, it would be fun for them to be able to read the book themselves.

The children will learn the ABCs together with the animals as well as learn something new about the alphabet and the animals.

Have fun!!!

ISBN: 9798371025418

Aa

I am the first letter in the alphabet. A is for alligator and also for the following animals:

Alligator

Antelope

Ant

Anteater

A
alligator

Bb

I am the second letter in the alphabet. B is for beaver and also for the following animals:

B

beaver

C c

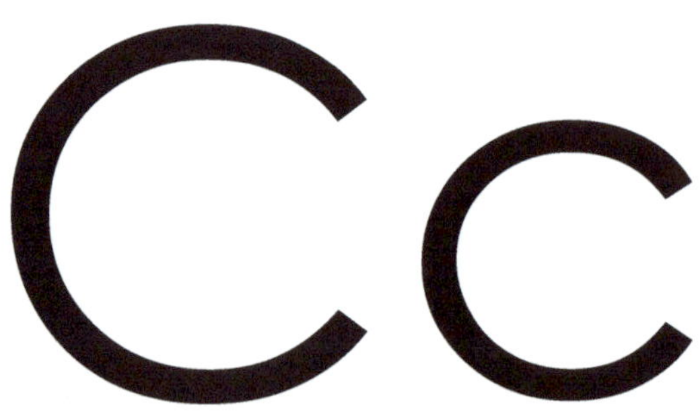

I am the third letter in the alphabet.

C is for cat and many other animals.

C
cat

D d

I am the fourth letter in the alphabet. D is for donkey.

D
donkey

Ee

I am the fifth letter in the alphabet. E is for elephant.

Eagle

Elk

Elephant

Eel

E
elephant

Ff

I am the sixth letter in the alphabet. F is for frog.

F

frog

G g

I am the seventh letter in the alphabet. G is for giraffe and many other animals..

G
giraffe

Hh

I am the eighth letter in the alphabet. H is for horse.

H
horse

Ii

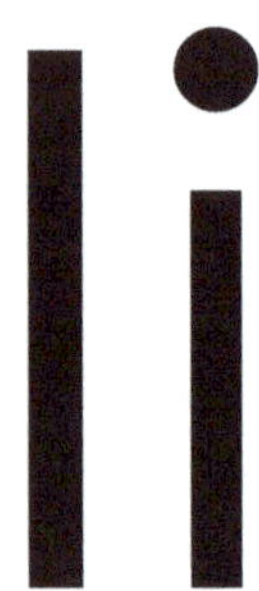 

I am the ninth letter in the alphabet. I is for iguana, and iguanas are excellent swimmers.

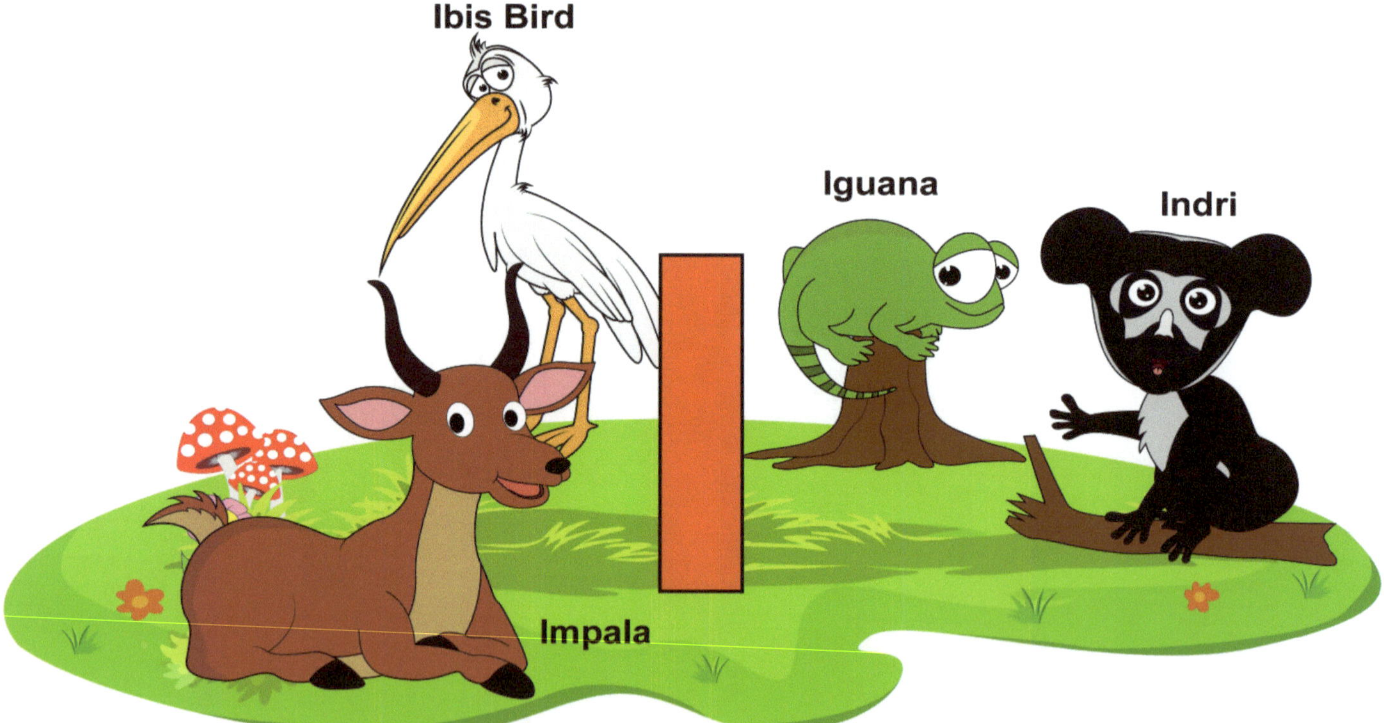

I
iguana

Jj

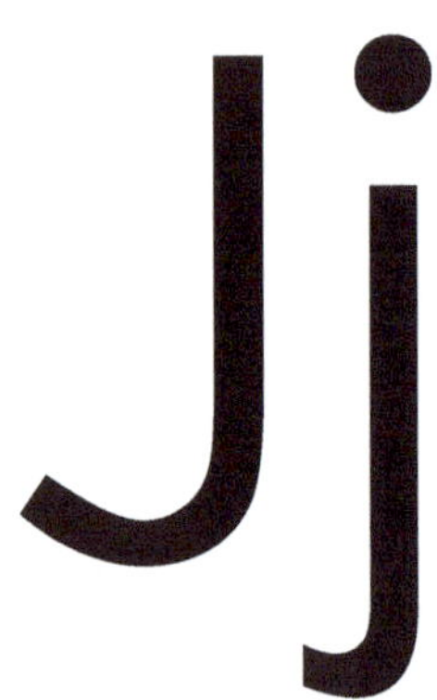

I am the tenth letter in the alphabet. J is for jellyfish, and a jellyfish is made up of **98%** water.

J

jellyfish

K k

I am the eleventh letter in the alphabet.

K is for kangaroo and many other animals.

K
kangaroo

Ll

I am the twelfth letter in the alphabet.

L is for lion and many other animals.

Ladybug

Lion

Lemur

Lizard

L
lion

Mm

I am the thirteenth letter in the alphabet. M is for mouse, and mice love cheese.

M
mouse

Nn

I am the fourteenth letter in the alphabet.

N is for numbat and many other animals.

N
numbat

Oo

I am the fifteenth letter in the alphabet.

O is for octopus and many other animals..

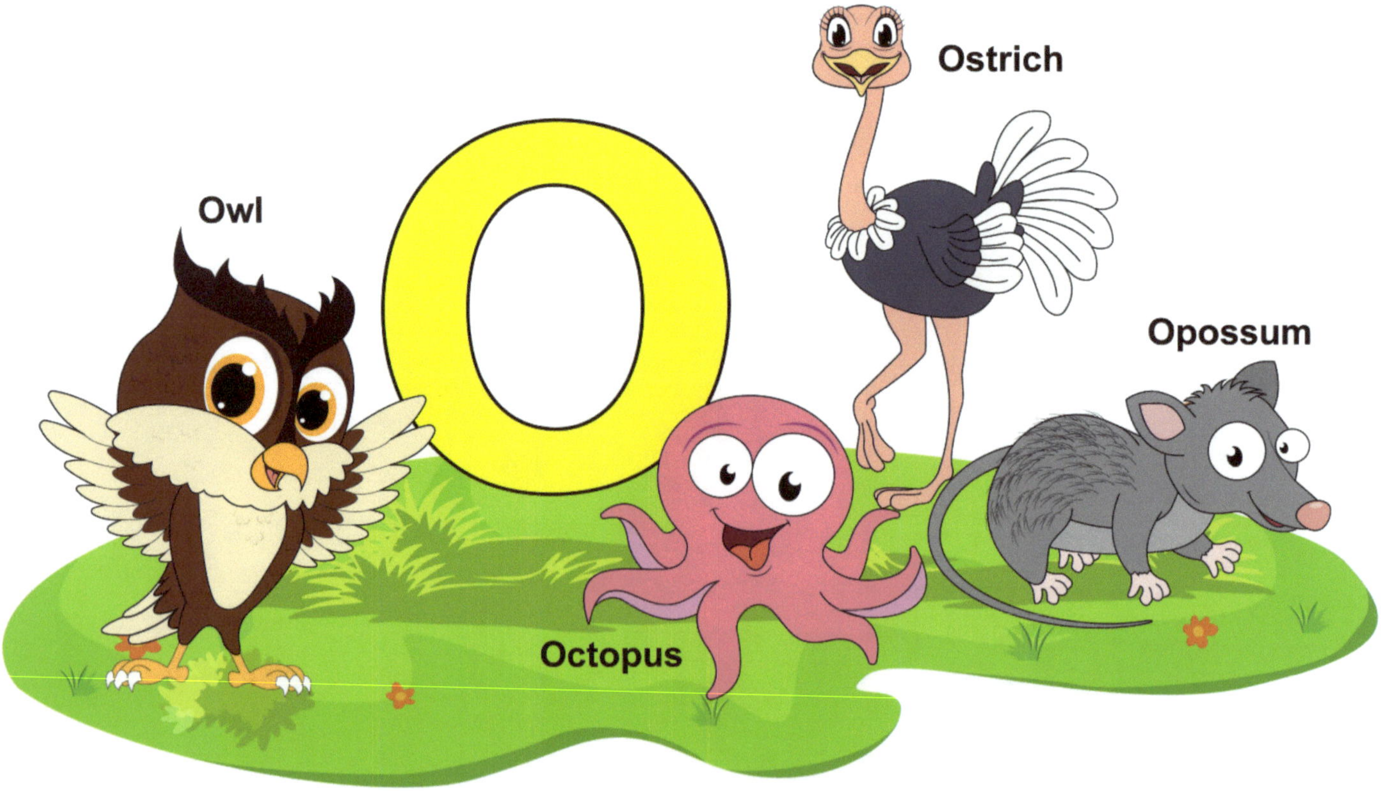

O

octopus

Pp

I am the sixteenth letter in the alphabet.

P is for panda and many other animals.

Porcupine

Panda

Peacock

Penguin

P
panda

Qq

I am the seventeenth letter in the alphabet.

Q is for quetzal and many other animals.

Q

quetzal

Rr

I am the eighteenth letter in the alphabet.

R is for raccoon and many other animals.

Rhinoceros

Raccoon

Rooster

Rabbit

R

raccoon

S s

I am the nineteenth letter in the alphabet.

S is for sheep and many other animals.

S
sheep

T t

I am the twentieth letter in the alphabet.

T is for turtle and many other animals.

T

turtle

U u

I am the twenty-first letter in the alphabet.

U is for unicorn and many other animals.

Urial

Unicorn

Uakari

Umbrella Bird

U
unicorn

V v

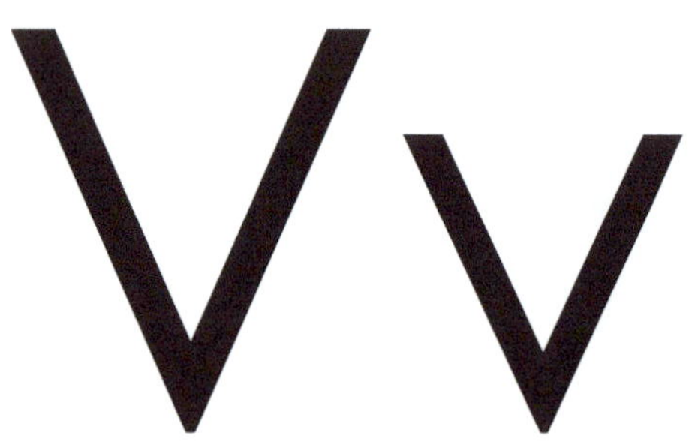

I am the twenty-second letter in the alphabet.

V is for viper and many other animals.

V
viper

W w

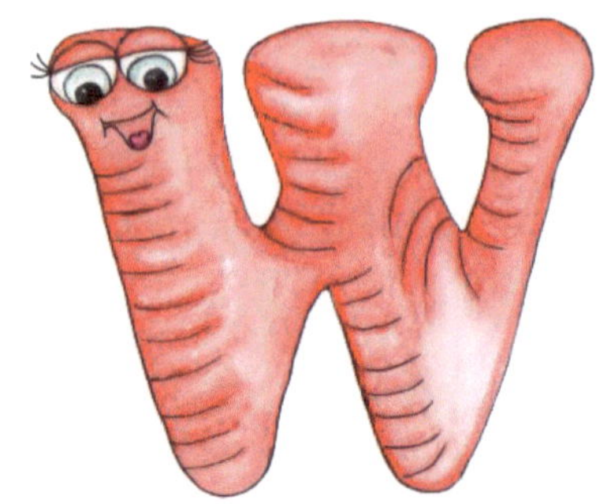

I am the twenty-third letter in the alphabet.

W is for whale and many other animals.

Wasp

Wolf

Warthog

Walrus

W

whale

Xx

I am the twenty-fourth letter in the alphabet.

X is for x-ray fish and many other animals.

X
x- ray fish

Yy

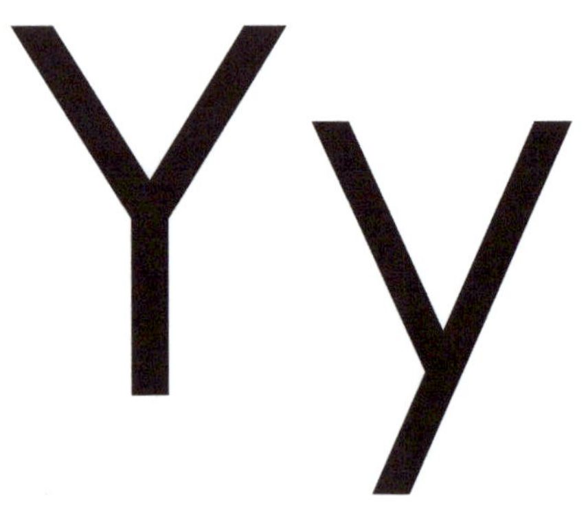

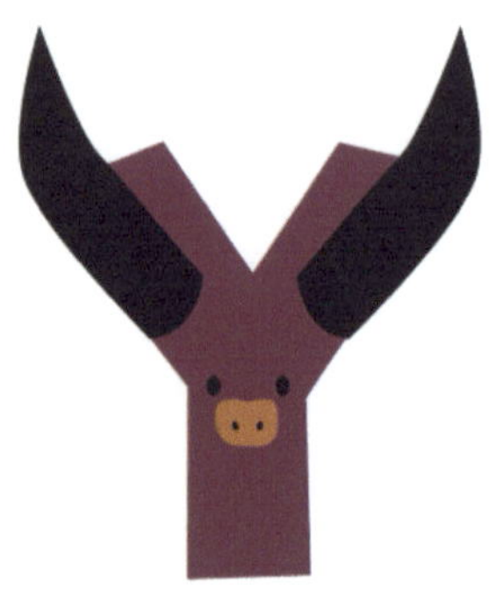

I am the twenty-fifth letter in the alphabet.

Y is for yak, and yaks are robust cattle with a large frame.

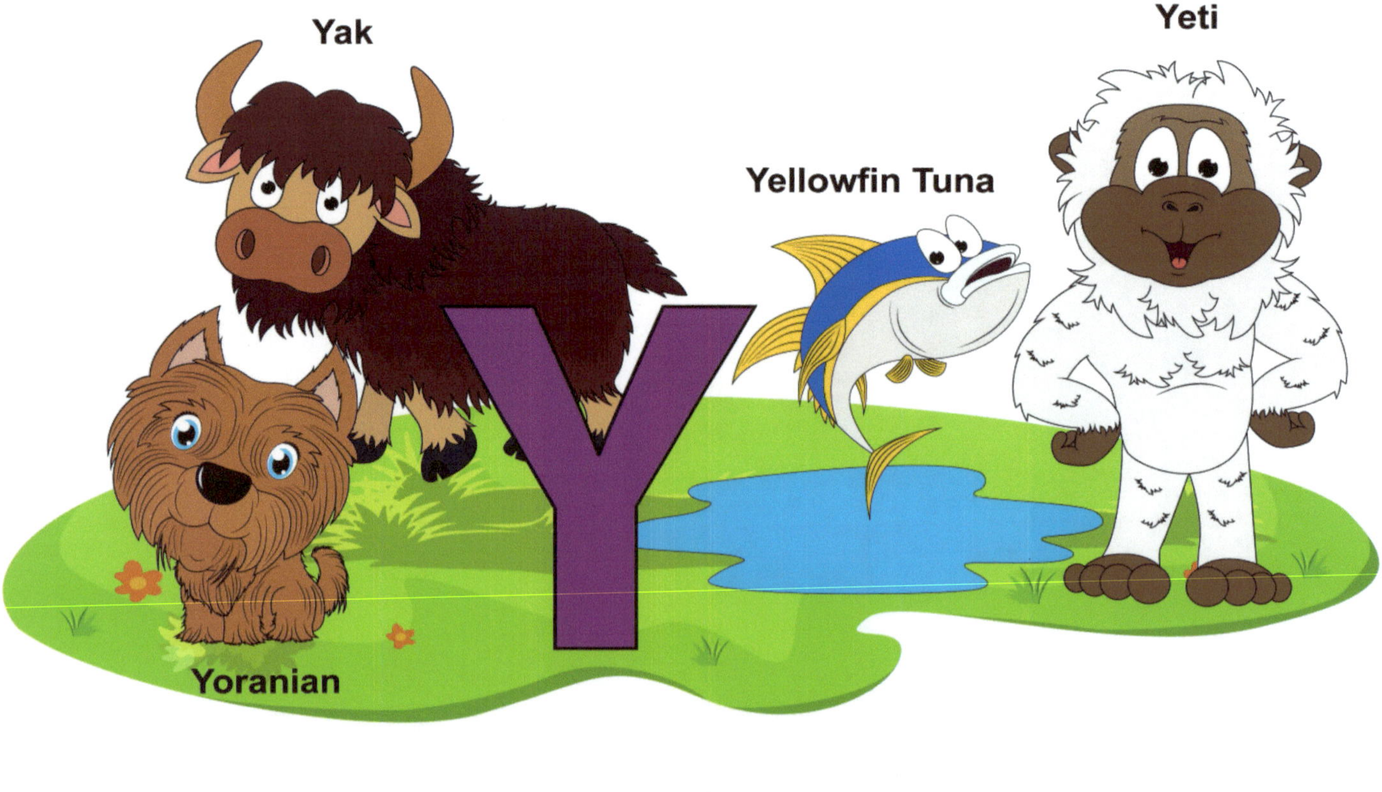

Yak

Yellowfin Tuna

Yeti

Yoranian

Y
yak

Zz

I am the twenty-sixth and last letter in the alphabet.

Z is for zebra, and zebras run very fast.

Z
zebra

IMPRINT

©2022, Dr. Obi Obata
Tarnowitzer Weg 85
68307 Mannheim - Germany
Publisher:Dr. Obi Obata, Independent Publisher
Contact: publication@women-at-work.org